The Doppler Effect

poems by

Marla Melito

Finishing Line Press
Georgetown, Kentucky

The Doppler Effect

ACKNOWLEDGMENTS

Thanks to the editors of *5th Gear, Greensboro Review, Phoebe, Gargoyle,* and
Roanoke Review where some of these poems first appeared.

Publisher: Leah Maines

Editor: Christen Kincaid

Cover Art: Tom LeGro

Author Photo: Megan Mumford

Cover Design: Elizabeth Maines

Printed in the USA on acid-free paper.
Order online: www.finishinglinepress.com
              also available on amazon.com

Author inquiries and mail orders:
Finishing Line Press
P. O. Box 1626
Georgetown, Kentucky 40324
U. S. A.

Table of Contents

For Andy, Watson, Penelope, and Lu

The Moondial

1.

You sat each night in your workshop, shivering,
Trying to make sense of the instructions that were not
Instructions, just the whispers of your mother's words.

Then, tired of winter, you packed your tools
And slipped under the equator, looking
For new material, new forms, new constellations,
But the moondial visited you at night.

At night, even after the last voice slipped into bed,
Its image rose in your dreams—it crept across the floor.
I never heard your terrified whispers scratch the page.

2.

The blueprints are locked in the drawer:
Circles, angles, smudges.
Try to deny its existence. I have seen it.

For all of January you distort the world with your telescope.
The lost eyelash on my cheek: the rim of the Milky Way.
The silence of the room: deep space.
You devote this new year to emptiness.

In Asunción the sky will be clearer.
We can map the moon; I will teach you.
I can read a key. I know north from south.
I know the distance to the moon and have measured the passing of time.

At the half moon you hint at the dial,
Your index finger throws shadows.
You claim you are an artist and this is your work.
I also know how to chart lies.

3.

You etch the moondial with bits of charcoal on granite.
You steal violets and hide tears.
Deny your mother rests here.
Tell me again how violets uproot and fall.

You think I do not see the half-moons under your eyes?
I have watched you study twilight walking through our yard—
The lavender shadow lighting your cheek.
You say you are studying. I know you are waiting.

The telescope, crumpled papers, bitten pencils,
The universe you choose.

4.

You have finished the first installment—
A white stone tablet and a circle of black paint.
It begins to chart the hours of the night;
You ache to chart the phases of the moon.

You claim you need to study from a new angle.
The words click into place with the latches on your suitcase.
I cannot fight with the moon; I no longer see you.

The new cycle begins tomorrow—
An eyelash of light flickers through the clouds.
I draw black circles on white parchment,
Tracking departures.

Red

I rest in every object,
Coiled and waiting.
It is not gold coins that give you strength,
But the gold hiss of my center,
The blue flicker of my choice.
I may stretch out before you, warming your hands and feet,
Drying your meaningless tears.
Your lover knew my force
After I singed her green robes.
She left flowers on my mantel;
I leave her three gold rings behind.
Do not tempt me with your pompous whiskers.
In an instant I can strike.
Turn to me and bow your head.

Jeremiah

I have tasted sand by force
Of a hand hidden in a fist.
I was fed muscle from beneath
Tiny pools of water and blood.
It wasn't enough to leave me alone,
Fired in the sun, glazed by the wind.
I needed to be placed into the flames
With anything that would burn.
Concentrate on melting the surface.
Make me weak enough to accept anything—
The smoke of newspapers, broken branches, old photographs.
Make me shine in reds and greens.
Let me forget the fists and the clay.

Late November

Window: an opening especially in the wall of a building

> We couldn't draw snow—
> instead we drew black X's on parchment.

At this hour, the sky is reflected back.
I like to watch the street.

> *for the admission of light and air*

> > We couldn't draw birds either—
> > just M's flapping in wax.

My neighbors watch me undress.
It doesn't help to use the blind.

> *closed by casement or sashes*

> > My best friend was blind.
> > During the summer, we would lie on the grass.

> *containing transparent material (as glass)*

I used to have a good body.
Look at me—don't you see it?

> > My friend was weak. She used a cane.
> > The boys on our street would look at her.

capable of being open and shut.

It is too late to go out. The windows
are black. No one is home.

> She moved away after the fire.
> That fall I would lay in ashes.

Pentimento

1.

What if—
beneath that swooping hand
a red barn peeks through
mistaken for a vein,
a mistaken stroke.

> There are no mistakes,
> there are accidents—
> the crash of white on canvas
> mixed with too much scarlet
> added to spirit the marble.

What if—
inside the red barn
two cows mourn
waiting for the rabbi
and a blessed stroke.

> Stroke: touch
> of the hand,
> glint of steel,
> dissatisfied
> veins.

What if—
the veins empty upside down in the barn,
the floor, thick and black, the rabbi's
back to the door, the book covered
by his white hand stained scarlet.

2.

Thick braids hang about her cheeks.
A pink dress, sweater, black shoes.
Her body pulled tight against her bones.

When I was that girl I thought I could reach my rib cage.
I thought I could turn my breastbone and give myself wings.
In my chest lived a raven cawing to get out.

3.

What if there were only
the superstition and the blessings?
Vietnam before the rainy season.
They hired the 25-year-old psychic to find their son.
She knew nothing of him but the trinkets they clutched
and the torn photograph from his childhood.

They wandered through fields looking for a sign—
screeching birds meant nothing. They only needed an egg
to balance on a chopstick. The father and mother had waited,
prayed the legend had to be right—they trusted
their son's spirit to the woman in pink pumps,
the woman they knew could be their granddaughter.

At the base of the tree the woman stopped and dropped the photograph
the mother had tentatively given her. The black and white smile
faded into the shadows. The father dropped to his knees.

Who exists when the physics of bombs cannot dispute
the balance of a small brown egg on a chopstick, the mother's
red eyes finding sleep? The father's white knuckles release.

4.

They took an x-ray of a broken bone,
looking for a changed mind, a fissure into the painter.

Her dress, the boundary between pink and red.
Were there flowers, really? Did she play the lute?

Sometimes things are covered for a reason.
Instead it takes a machine (in black and white)

to cut through the strokes and paint, to uncover
the painter's apparent original intent.

If they took an x-ray of her chest, would it find an error?
If they touched her hand, would they find marble?

Angkor Wat

The path digs into the ground
One foot in front of another.
Two children walk in the center.
They fear grass and point to the edge.

The one-armed girl shakes her head
As her brother ties her boot. He is rare—
His four limbs huddled against
His stomach as he crouches by her foot.

It is Tuesday and the noon sun hides
The shadows of the temple
And the children. Wait for the flash
Of the camera. The woman in black
Gives them money and smiles.
She turns to photograph the cracked steps.

Inside the temple, they pray and offer incense,
Then turn to walk back to the path.
An old woman, leaning on a crutch, watches
The boy's winged shadow stretch from the path
As he reaches for his sister's left arm.

The Burqa

She stands, a pillar of black against the gray tide—
One toe to the world, one toe in defiance.

Further up from the sea, the same girl, or a different girl,
Bleeds through her veil, bleeds onto black.

For showing her eyes, they dragged her to the stadium
And beat her until her head bobbed like a snapped tulip wrapped in black.

At the hospital for women there was nothing
To stop the pooling black on black.

Behind the painted windows and sealed doors
A mother's veil pores over black and white photos.

The living shrouded as the dead, the dead walk among the living.
Up this river, there is no wind—only the hush of black.

The Accidental Occurrence

The challenge lies not in finding birds, but also in accurately identifying each bird seen.

—Guide to North American Birds

It was an accidental occurrence,
The square-tailed swallow that rose from the trees.
There should never have been this disturbance,

In meadows where he studied in silence—
Where he concentrated on what should be.
There was an accidental occurrence.

He knew the calls, the songs, the patterns,
But flesh and blood were not addressed in key.
There should never have been this disturbance.

But too naïve and proud to seek assurance,
He stared at the cave swallow above him, free.
It was an accidental occurrence

That this bold bird defied the map and boundaries.
It did not inherit predictability—
There should never be this type of disturbance.

Instead he took a rock, and with no deterrence,
His anger fired. The bird did not think to flee.
It was an accidental occurrence.

Its body dropped with self-assurance.
His eyes darkened and stared blankly.
It was an accidental occurrence—
There should never have been this disturbance.

The Answer Is (Always) in the Equation

Source
You babble to the plane
trying to make yourself
larger than the spot you occupy.
You wish you were a star or circle.

Sound is never constant—
just listen to your voice.
You are a point
to be judged by.

Force[3]
Sitting under a table
of gutters and clouds,
the plane shakes your words
out of earshot.
Or was it your words
rattling its path?

Velocity
Dropping an egg
in the center of the kitchen
is another story. Cracking a hearth…

Talk to the one-legged girl,
ask her what she sees.
Nothing and more of the same.

Force²
The river flows harder in the spring
swimming faster and faster from the land.
He jumps from boat to boat
hands, pies, shirt-tails waving to the shore.

Buy, buy! he shouts to
greenbacks basking in the sun.
He knows he is a bird,
collecting twigs, scooping up worms.

Velocity²
She watched her father
slide down the white
walls of the classroom
from a certain bullet.

She is forty-seven,
the only one left from her family
to carry sticks to the fire.

The pyre has cooled.
She has no questions for them.
The only controversy, they say,
Were there fourteen or sixteen doctors left?
She is one. Her father was two.

+/-
Light of the moon
Swim in the fields
Light of the fire
Weep in the hearth
Light of the hearth—

We stood at the beginning
and did nothing.

Light of the moon
Light of the hearth

-/+

It would be easier to destroy
a book if we could prove the evil
of Einstein's typing—if we could try
the mind of Newton and find it treasonous.
Why should there be so much defined?
Why should there be anything more than
simple math and apples?

Velocity of Object
When did the sirens ring flames
and desks become shelter?
Why does the quiet girl hate us?

We were Prometheus bringing light.
No one said it would be less.

=

The only constant is light
and that is all there is to say.
Your questions vary in frequency,
but never in size. You are small.
Your mind is a sleeping swimmer.

Stay small (lightning only strikes
the tall). Crouch in the grass,
listen for the river. When you hear it,
bury your forehead.

Electricity is drawn to water—
you must wait to dive.

Origin

The weeping willow tells no secrets
as the storm tears its branches.
The light from the house holds still,
quieted by the rain.
(Light gives and takes through the yard.
Thunder leaves nothing but its echo.)
In the house a family breaks
bread and lights candles.
In the morning they will count the rings
of the split willow's trunk.

Translation

Silk sleeves fall silent,
Dust covers the jade courtyard,
Rooms now cold and still.

Leaves rot on closed doors.
Waiting for you, beautiful moon,
Feel my heart breaking.

Marla Melito was born and raised in North Adams, Massachusetts and lived for many years in the DC area, where she was a member of DC WritersCorps and a writer-in-residence for the DC Creative Writing Workshop. She has worked in international public health, taught English as a Second Language in Costa Rica, and taught literature, composition, and poetry workshops at George Mason University, where she earned her MFA in Creative Writing. She lives in upstate NY.